Astrology

WISDOM OF THE STARS

By the Same Author

Dreams
Drums, Rattles, and Bells
Flutes, Whistles, and Reeds
Gliders
Haunted Houses
Investigating UFO's
Kites
Magic Made Easy
Puzzle Patterns
Religions East and West
Shadows
Singing Strings
Sixth Sense
Song, Speech, and Ventriloquism
Spinning Tops
Spooky Magic

Astrology
WISDOM OF THE STARS
Larry Kettelkamp

with illustrations by the author
William Morrow and Company
New York   1973

Library of Congress Catalog Card Number 73-4924
ISBN 0-688-20085-0
ISBN 0-688-30085-5 (lib. bdg.)

4 5 77 76

The author wishes to thank
the following persons
for offering helpful suggestions:

Mr. Bill Stillwagon,
Training Instructor,
RCA Space Center,
Princeton, New Jersey,
and independent teacher-astrologist

Dr. J. M. Holman,
Manager Mission Analysis,
RCA Space Laboratories,
Princeton, New Jersey

Contents

Astrology
WISDOM OF THE STARS

Introduction

The idea that a revelation of truth could be found in the patterns of the heavenly bodies is as old as mankind. To the ancients it seemed clear that events in the heavens were reflected in the actions of men on earth and that the heavens controlled their destinies. The world of men, therefore, was linked with the larger universe, each being part of a whole, and nothing could happen in either sphere without affecting the other. Thus, the study of the heavens always has been very important. Astrology, meaning "star wisdom," was the first science of the skies, and it is still with us today.

In time, a division occurred between those who wanted to interpret the sky patterns as they were believed to affect human destiny and those who tried to look at the stars and planets objectively, believing that they could not influence the affairs of men who had free will and free choice. The objectivists began to distinguish their study as astronomy, meaning "star discipline." But all the pioneer astronomers from Copernicus to Kepler were also astrologers.

Does astrology work? Millions of people around the world who study their sun signs or who have had horoscopes drawn up believe it works very well indeed. Others, including many scientists, think it is nothing but superstition. However, a small number of pioneer scientists are making new discoveries in astrobiology, studying the ways in which radiation and magnetism from space affect people on earth and as they travel in space. Surprisingly, these new discoveries are much like some of the ideas of traditional astrology.

I
Early Astrology

The First Horoscopes

The word horoscope literally means "hour observation" and is a forecast of the future based on the positions of the heavenly bodies at birth. At first those who studied the stars were interested in the way the heavens seemed to foretell the changing seasons, the changing weather, and events of great importance. Since such events were apt to concern the fates of kings and nations, astrologers began to busy themselves with foretelling the fortunes of royalty.

In an early message written by a Babylonian astrologer to his king there is a warning about an oncoming eclipse, which usually was interpreted as an evil omen. The king is advised to perform certain religious rites. As it turned out, the weather was cloudy and the eclipse could not be seen. The astrologer later writes, "The great gods who live in the city of your Majesty have covered up the sky and not shown the eclipse. That is what the King should know; that this eclipse has no relation to your Majesty or his Country."

Because of the attempts to predict the fate of nations and the moods of the gods, the signs in the heavens became more and more important. Animals and gods of all sorts were associated with particular planets or configurations of stars, and the sun and moon as well.

In time, horoscopes, based on interpreting the sky signs at the time of birth, became popular for individuals. Good and bad influences were associated with various heavenly bodies; many of them still are accepted by astrologers today. A child born when the moon had come forth was supposed to be bright, with a regular and long life. The influence also would be good if he were born under the sun or Jupiter; he would live a long, healthy life and would grow rich. However, if a child was born when Saturn had come forth, then his life would be dark with hardships.

The reading of horoscopes came more and more to depend on those particular constellations that were crossed by the sun, moon, and planets as they gradually changed positions in the sky. And so the idea of the zodiac developed.

How the Zodiac Began

As the earth revolves around the sun, the sun appears to move slowly across the background of stars, taking a year to return to its starting place. This apparent path of the sun forms a belt across the sky. The star groups visible along or near this path were of great interest to those who studied the heavens— hence the name zodiac, a Greek word meaning "circle of figures" or "circle of life." The Chaldeans called the path "Anu's way," after one of the Babylonian gods. In addition to the sun, the moon and the planets as seen from the earth also appeared to move along this pathway. Early Babylonian mathematicians divided the period from sunrise to sunrise into twelve equal parts, using certain constellations of stars along the sun's path as markers. Each star group was alloted one twelfth of the circle, or thirty degrees. It took about one "hour" of 120 minutes, as the Babylonians figured it, for each thirty-degree section of sky, or sign, to rise above the horizon during the day-night period. Our time measurements still follow those of the Babylonians, although we divide each Babylonian hour into two so that a day contains twenty-four hours instead of twelve.

The Babylonian zodiac was borrowed first by the Greeks and then by the Romans. Although the names of the figures have changed, the signs and the twelve-part division have been retained. These signs circling the sky, still called the zodiac, are visible to viewers over most of the globe during the year and are particularly familiar in the northern hemisphere, where their names and traditions originated.

Some of the earliest writings about the zodiac are attributed to the Egyptian, Hermes Trismegistus. It is not known whether Hermes was an actual person or simply one of the great gods of the ancient Egyptians. In Egypt he was called Thoth, and later he shared the name of the Greek god, Hermes. The early Greek writers on astrology credit Hermes as being the source of wisdom in such matters. Many

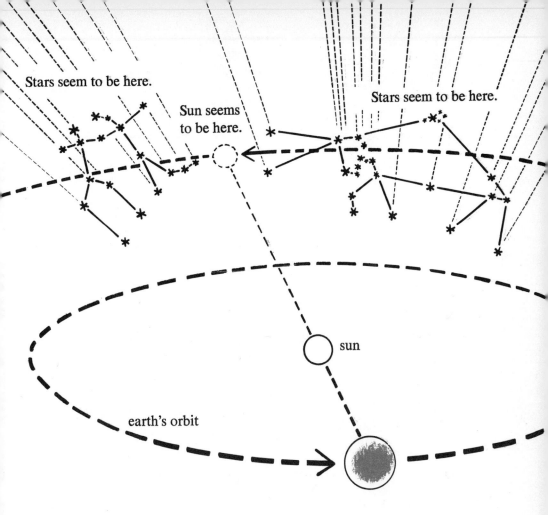

Stars seem to be here.

Sun seems to be here.

Stars seem to be here.

sun

earth's orbit

As seen from the earth, distant star images seem to form patterns across the sky. As earth revolves around the sun, the sun seems to move slowly along the constellations of the zodiac.

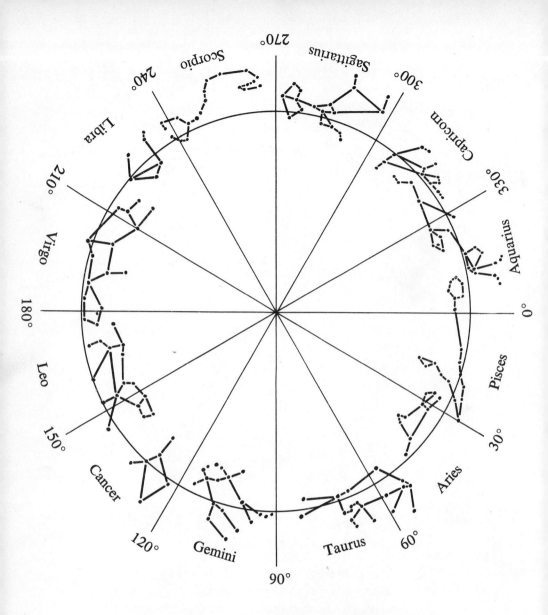

The constellations of the zodiac appear in a circle along the apparent path of the sun, with the sky divided into twelve 30° sections. 0° marks the present location of the sun on the first day of spring.

books attributed to Hermes, such as the *Sacred Book of Hermes, Medical Mathematics,* and the *Book of Hermes on the Plants of the Seven Planets,* were passed along from one generation to the next. Hermes was believed to be the original authority on medicine, botany, mathematics, and the influence of the stars and planets in all of these studies. If Hermes did live and if he wrote even part of what is credited to him, he was one of the world's first great scientists. It is remarkable how complete these ideas were then and how little they have changed over the centuries.

Early in the first century A.D., a Roman named Manilius wrote five books of poetry on astrology called the *Astronomicon.* Presented in a popular style, it is a summary of the earlier Egyptian and Greek books. Manilius emphasized two ideas that have since become part of modern astrology. The first was that each of the twelve signs of the zodiac matches a part of the human body. Imagine a human figure bent in a curve around the zodiac. The head begins in the sign Aries the Ram, the neck and shoulders are in the sign of Taurus the Bull, and so on around the circle until one reaches the feet in the last sign of Pisces the Fish.

The second idea made popular by Manilius was that of houses. Wherever you were when you were born, one particular zodiacal sign was rising above the horizon. This section of sky was called the first house, and the rising sign was called the ascendant. The next section of sky to rise was the second house, and so on, until all twelve sections, or houses, had passed overhead during twenty-four hours. Each house was thought to have a special influence over the events of a person's private life.

The name Ptolemy is known to every student of astronomy or astrology. Claudius Ptolemy was a Greek who lived in Alexandria, Egypt, in the second century A.D. He became a mathematician and developed a theory of planetary motions that was taught for hundreds of years. Ptolemy believed the earth was in the center of the universe, and sun and moon revolved around it. The planets must too then, but there Ptolemy encountered a perplexing problem. Seen from the earth, the planets sometimes appear to move forward in the sky in the same direction as the sun and moon, sometimes to stand still, and at other times to move backward among the fixed stars. For this reason the Greeks named these lights in the sky planets, which means "wanderers."

Ptolemy worked out an ingenious explanation of these strange motions. He assumed that the planets traveled in circular paths around the earth but that they moved in small circles around their main orbits as they went along. In this way, he thought, they would at times seem to stand still or move backward. Ptolemy presented his mathematical model of the solar system in his famous work, the *Amalgest*.

But Ptolemy was also an astrologer: every object in the heavens and every motion must have a meaning. His *Tetrabiblos*, or *Four Books on the Influence of the Stars*, has become the basic reference for astrologers from Ptolemy's day to the present. Since most scholars and scientists accepted Ptolemy's model of the solar system for centuries, people everywhere also believed his *Tetrabiblos* to be the best source of astrological interpretation.

Ptolemy's books on astrology gathered together the ideas current among the earlier Greeks. How the planets and stars were believed to affect each individual was outlined in detail. The influence of a planet was supposed to blend with that of the sign it was passing through. Those born under a certain planet would tend to have particular physical features associated with it. For example, Saturn, ascendant, was said to make people dark-skinned and robust, with black curly hair, and their temperaments would be "moist and cold." However, if the planet were setting, those born would be straight-haired and graceful, and their temperaments would be "cold and dry."

When the Romans conquered Greece, they adopted many of the Greek concepts. The Romans originally had their own way of fortune-telling: omens were read from various phenomena such as lightning and thunder, the flight of birds, or the examination of organs of sacrificed animals. At first those who practiced the old Chaldean methods of reading the future from the stars were scorned by the Romans who thought them superstitious and uneducated. In 139 B.C. the Emperor Hispallus even tried to banish Chaldean astrologers from the kingdom. But astrology was popular, and, far from disappearing, it became increasingly accepted by the common people.

Finally the philosopher Posidonius, a respected

teacher in Rome, announced that astrology was a
genuine science. Then the nobility grew interested,
and a new group of scholars began to take up astrology. Astrologers came to be highly respectable, their
advice was sought at every birth and before every
important undertaking. The emperors Octavius and
Tiberius consulted astrologers. And so, by the time
of Augustus Caesar, astrology had become a part of
daily life.

With the barbarian invasions and the fall of
the Roman Empire, most of the books and ideas of
the civilizations of the ancient world were lost. In
the centuries that followed, many theories about
astrology disappeared along with teachings in mathematics and philosophy. Beliefs in omens, magic,
demons, and spells were common. Simple books of
signs and omens appeared. The Church was the
keeper of what learning survived, and the emphasis
was on religious faith rather than on science. Ptolemy's model of the earth-centered universe, which
seemed in agreement with the Bible, was accepted
without much question.

Learning, science, and the arts still flourished in
the Arab world, however. Arab libraries preserved

many Greek writings lost to Europe until the exciting period of rediscovery known as the Renaissance, which took its name from the French word meaning "rebirth." Then scholars fought for the freedom to present ideas whether or not they were acceptable to the Church and the ruling classes.

Renaissance Astronomy and Astrology

In 1543, the astronomer Nicholas Copernicus published his famous work, *The Revolutions of the Heavenly Spheres*. He revived an idea held by a few of the early Greeks that the earth and the other planets revolve around the sun. Attempts to explain planetary movements with Ptolemy's system had resulted in complicated diagrams of circles of all sizes. Although Ptolemy's system had fit the facts of observation, Copernicus's theory also fit the observations and was much simpler in addition. Accordingly, it became the basis of modern astronomy.

But Copernicus and his fellow-astronomers were astrologers as well. They believed that the patterns they found in the sky must influence the lives of men. Their hope was to understand human affairs better by studying the exact motions of the stars and planets.

One of these men was the Danish astronomer, Tycho Brahe, who produced a theory of the solar system that was a combination of Ptolemy's and Copernicus's. The earth was in the center, and the sun and moon went around it in circles. However, the rest of the planets were shown orbiting around the sun. Tycho Brahe's measurements of the movements of the planets, made over a period of twenty years, were extremely exact, and he became famous for them.

The young astronomer Johannes Kepler went to work as an assistant to Tycho Brahe in his observatory. Although Kepler believed that Copernicus was right in placing the sun in the center of the planets and so did not agree with Brahe's system, he was much impressed with the methods used at the observatory. After the death of Tycho Brahe, Kepler succeeded him as court mathematician to the em-

Johannes Kepler, who discovered that the planets travel in ellipses around the sun, theorized that angles between other planets and the earth affect the weather.

peror and acquired the observatory records kept by the Danish astronomer over the years.

In particular, Brahe had collected the most accurate measurements ever made of the positions of Mars in its orbit around the sun. Kepler used Brahe's measurements and tried to draw the planetary orbits so that geometrical shapes such as the square, triangle, and hexagon would fit between them. These shapes did not fit exactly. One problem was that Brahe's measurements indicated that the orbit of Mars was not a perfect circle.

Kepler first tried drawing the orbit of Mars in the shape of an egg. When this did not work, he finally hit upon the shape of the ellipse. Kepler's solution was profoundly important, for it led to the discovery that all of the planetary orbits were ellipses and not perfect circles.

Like most of the astronomers of the time, Tycho Brahe believed that events on earth were influenced by the cycles of the heavenly bodies. At first Kepler, interested only in the mathematics of Brahe's observations, suspected that the Dane's astrology was just a pastime. So he decided to investigate on his own to prove that there was nothing to astrology.

One of Brahe's beliefs was that Mars influenced business affairs. Accordingly, Kepler plotted the timing of the nearest approaches of Mars and decided that, after all, the rise and fall of business activity in Germany did seem related to this cycle. He also concluded that the seven and one-half month period it took Venus to go around the sun was related to cycles of disease epidemics. Having started as a sceptic, Kepler became convinced that there must be some truth in astrology after all and began to explore astrological relationships more deeply. His book,

The Fundamentals of Astrology, collected his observations and conclusions.

Kepler also tried to find correlations between the
weather and planetary angles. In this research he em-
ployed the old Greek concept of aspects. Two planets
might be on opposite sides of the earth, lined up in a
straight line, making a 180-degree angle with the
earth. Or they might form a square corner with the
earth, an angle of 90 degrees, or perhaps the corner
of a perfect triangle, an angle of 60 degrees. These
planetary angles, or aspects, were believed to influence events on earth. Traditionally some angles were
favorable, some unfavorable, and others could be
either.

Kepler kept a weather diary for eight years and
believed he found some correspondence. "If two
planets stand at 89 degrees from one another, nothing will happen in the air," he wrote. "But tomorrow,
when the full square of 90 degrees is reached, a
thunderstorm will suddenly arise. The effect, therefore, does not come from a single star, but from the
angle, from the harmonious segment of the circle."
Kepler's conclusions about astrology were later dis-
missed by most scientists. Recently, however, a few

researchers have begun again to explore the relationship between planetary angles and changes on the
sun and the earth.

Famous Astrologers

In addition to those astrologers who were also astronomers, there always have been those who at-
tempted only to interpret the signs of the heavens.
All through the history of the Babylonians, the Egyptians, the Greeks, and the Romans, foretelling the
future was connected with religion. Many astrologers
were also priests who tried to foresee the fates of men
by means of divination, the art of discovering that
which is divine. It was thought that the plans of the
gods were revealed to those priests who understood
the signs and who had special powers.

Old Testament prophets were said to be able to
read the signs of the heavens in order to foresee the
future. The wise men who came to honor the birth
of Jesus in the New Testament are described as as-

trologers from the East. Apparently they had seen a bright sign in the sky and interpreted it to mean that a religious leader had been born. Actually the astrologers might have seen a conjunction of several planets lined up with a star so that they appeared at about the same spot in the sky. Such a conjunction did occur several years before Christ's birth.

Probably the most famous prophet astrologer of all time was the Frenchman Michel de Nostredame, better known as Nostradamus, who lived in the sixteenth century. He received an excellent education that included a medical degree. In addition to being a respected doctor, Nostradamus studied astrology. Soon he found he had a gift for intuitively sensing future events. It is said that once when Nostradamus was traveling in Italy, he suddenly knelt before a young monk who was a stranger to him saying, "I kneel before his Holiness." Although those present laughed at the time, many years later the same young monk became Pope Sistus V.

Nostradamus composed more than nine hundred small verses that predicted various political and social events. Skeptics say that Nostradamus's poems were written in such a puzzling style that they are almost impossible to understand. Believers point out that this style was typical of the times and ensured that serious writings would not be misinterpreted by uneducated readers.

Once one understands the style, most of the meanings appear quite clear. Part of the difficulty in interpreting Nostradamus occurs when his predictions cover events that have not yet happened. A statement that seems to make no sense before an event sometimes can be understood afterward. The writings of Nostradamus have been studied carefully by the English scholar, Stuart Robb, who concluded there is evidence of genuine predictive ability. In his studies Robb used only those books of verse published before the events the verses describe.

Nostradamus used word substitutes and sometimes disguised the name of a person or place by scrambling the letters of the name. He referred to England as the Island, or Neptune (god of the sea), and even called it "Great Brittain" before there was such a name. He referred to a ruler who might well be Napoleon, calling him Pau Nay Loron. Unscrambled, this anagram could stand for the French Napoleon Roy, or Napoleon the King.

In a typical verse, Nostradamus predicted the end
of Napoleon's power:

> The captive prince, conquered to Elba
> He will pass Genoa by sea to Marseilles.
> He is completely conquered
>   by a great effort of foreign forces,
> Though he escapes the flames,
>   the bees yield liquor by the barrel.

Nostradamus was quite specific. Napoleon was the
only French ruler to use the bee as an emblem of
power. When captured, Napoleon was exiled to the
Island of Elba. He did escape by boat as Nostradamus seems to have predicted but was captured
again. And though his life was saved, his defeat was
final.

Nostradamus also apparently predicted the fire of
London in 1666:

> The blood of the just
>   shall be required of London
> Burned by fire in thrice twenty and six;
> The old dame shall fall from her high place

Prophet-astrologer Nostradamus published poems predicting many details of the careers of future famous political leaders.

And many edifices of the same sect
shall be destroyed.

The word *dame* referred to the famous Cathedral of Notre Dame in Paris. In the fire, Saint Paul's Cathedral and other churches were destroyed.

Stuart Robb and others used Nostradamus's verses to predict events of World War II. Nostradamus described the fall of the French line of defense and the taking of Paris. He referred to a man named Hister.

Hister was not only similar to Hitler but was an ancient name for the Danube River, suggesting that the dictator was Austrian, as Hitler was.

Some of Nostradamus's predictions for the future are more puzzling. He wrote, "There will be a head of London from the government of America," something which certainly has not happened yet. And in an astrological verse about France in the year 1999, which is not yet understood, he said:

> In the year 1999 in the seventh month,
> A great king of frightfulness will come
>   from the skies
> To revive the great king of Angoumois;
> Around this time Mars will reign
>   for the good cause.

Although many critics continue to argue that the verses of Nostradamus can be interpreted to fit almost any situation, others remain convinced that the French astrologer clearly read the keys to the future and passed them along to mankind.

In the seventeenth century the English astrologer William Lilly wrote a book called, *Christian Astrol-*

Astrologer William Lilly
predicted accurately
the great fire of London,
which occurred in 1666.

ogy Modestly Treated in Three Volumes. In it he
made astrological predictions for both kings and
commoners, some of which were remarkably accurate. About King Charles I, he said that because the
moon was near the star Antares, a reddish star that
looks like the planet Mars, and Antares meant blood
and violence, and because Mars itself was in a position which denoted "beheading," the king would meet
this kind of fate. Two years later King Charles was
indeed beheaded. Like Nostradamus, Lilly described
the great fire of London of 1666 before it happened.

He had been so specific that the Parliament sent a committee to investigate him, thinking that he might have caused the fire. Lilly was declared innocent and later turned to the practice of medicine, using astrology as a basis for his treatments.

Throughout the late Middle Ages and the Renaissance, astrology enjoyed great respect. Courses in astrology were taught at large universities alongside mathematics and the arts. However, in 1666, the French Academy of Science was founded. At that time the Church was attacking the sciences, including astrology, which were teaching ideas that upset Church doctrine. Accordingly, the French king was persuaded to exclude astrologers from the French Academy. Astronomers at the Academy of Sciences were forbidden the study of astrology. Elsewhere in Europe the importance of astrology began to be questioned and the truth of its principles placed in doubt. The perfection of the telescope caused astronomers to become more interested in what could be seen at great distances. The universe appeared to be immense. Many of the stars were found to be so far away that there seemed little chance of any of them affecting human life.

At the same time the development of the micro-scope allowed scientists to see smaller and smaller cells and particles of matter. Science began to divide into those who were looking into the distances of space and those examining the minute details of plants and animals on earth. Everyone agreed that the large objects in space were linked together by gravitational attraction, but most scientists could not believe that little men on the tiny planet earth, no more than a speck among the stars, could be influ-enced by objects so far away.

The excitement of so many new discoveries in a relatively short time awakened a new interest in logic and reason, which in turn strengthened the idea of free will. Religious thinkers and philosophers felt that by developing practical tools and machines, men could exercise choice and shape themselves and the world as they saw fit. People were less at the mercy of the elements around them and less inclined to in-vest them with divine powers. They were no longer in awe of what they could measure and understand. And so, although astrology never disappeared alto-gether, it ceased to be respected among people who relied on reason rather than intuition.

II
Traditional Astrology

Today astrology is enjoying a surge of popularity once again. Interest in the subject was revived at the beginning of the twentieth century, when two French scholars published comprehensive books on astrology. One was *Greek Astrology* by Bouché-Leclerq, and the other *Manual of Spherical and Judiciary Astrology* by Formalhaut. Both books attracted much attention. After the turmoil of World War I and the economic uncertainty that followed it, more and more people turned to astrology. In the 1930's astrological forecasts began to appear in newspapers. Popular books on astrology appeared in England and the United States, and the astrologers Alan Leo, Isabelle Pagan, and Evangeline Adams wrote books that became well known. Numerous writers followed in their footsteps.

Astrological societies have sprung up in many countries. In England the Faculty of Astrological

Studies grants a diploma to students of astrology. The American Federation of Astrologers, which has its headquarters in Washington, D.C., and affiliate organizations throughout the country suggest a code of ethics and list members in good standing.

Today one can hear astrologers on the radio and on television. The newsstands are full of paperback books on astrology, some of them best sellers. Many books and pamphlet series deal mainly with day-to-day predictions and advice based on the sun sign, or astrological month of birth.

The sun has moved back about two zodiacal signs over the last 4000 years, so astrological dates below show the sun's symbolic location rather than the true position.

Aries Mar 21- Apr 19	Taurus Apr 20- May 20	Gemini May 21- June 20	Cancer June 21- Jul 22	Leo Jul 23- Aug 22	Virgo Aug 23- Sept 22
Libra Sept 23- Oct 22	Scorpio Oct 23- Nov 21	Sagittarius Nov 22- Dec 21	Capricorn Dec 22- Jan 19	Aquarius Jan 20- Feb 18	Pisces Feb 19- Mar 20

The same birth-month system is used in the columns of the daily papers. The assumption is that everyone born, say, between April 20 and May 20, under the sign of Taurus the Bull, will tend to be influenced the same way on the same day. If one compares several columns written by different astrologers for the same day and sun sign, however, one is apt to find conflicting predictions. According to one paper, Tuesday for the Taurus person might be "a good day to relax and get away from pressures. Avoid making important decisions at this time. Visit a close friend." In a newspaper column written by another astrologer, Taurus people may be told to "take stock of your assets. Do not put off those important decisions. Take advantage of your energy surplus to get things started. This is a good day to go out and meet new people."

Studies of such columns show that there is little or no consistency among them. And it seems unlikely that millions of people born in different years but in the same thirty-day period should all heed the same advice on the same day even if the astrologers could agree on the best advice to give them. Part of the success of these simple columns is that much of the advice is so general that the reader can interpret it to suit himself. Often a column suggests several alternatives. "Watch out for small accidents today. With care these can be avoided." Whether or not an accident happens to the reader, the astrologer is safe. And no one would argue that being careful is bad advice.

At the other extreme is a complete birth chart and horoscope prepared by an experienced astrologer, often for a substantial fee. The client supplies the place of birth, along with the day and year and the time down to the hour and minute if possible. Taking into account the latitude and longitude of the place of birth and time zones, the astrologer then refers to an ephemeris, a book of exact tables that show in which signs the sun, moon, and planets are located at any one time to the precise degree. The planetary positions given are accurate for a particular section of sky. Since the sun gradually shifts against the background of constellations about one sign every 2000 years, however, the actual positions of sun, moon, and planets are now about two signs behind those listed in the tables. The exact time of birth is important because a different sign of the zodiac rises every two hours and the ascending sign is one part of the birth chart.

The professional astrologer produces a complex-looking circular birth chart with compartments, labels, constellation signs, planet positions, and angle notations. The chart will look about the same no matter who prepares it since it is a map of the sky, so to speak, showing the relative positions of heavenly bodies for one time and place. In interpretation, however, the astrologer will follow certain general rules combined with his own insights according to his own experience.

Casting a Horoscope

The easiest way to understand what a horoscope is all about is to draw up your own. You can start with yourself and then try it on friends or relatives.

1. Check the birth-date chart on page 46 to find the sign the sun was assigned to when you were born. This is your sun sign.

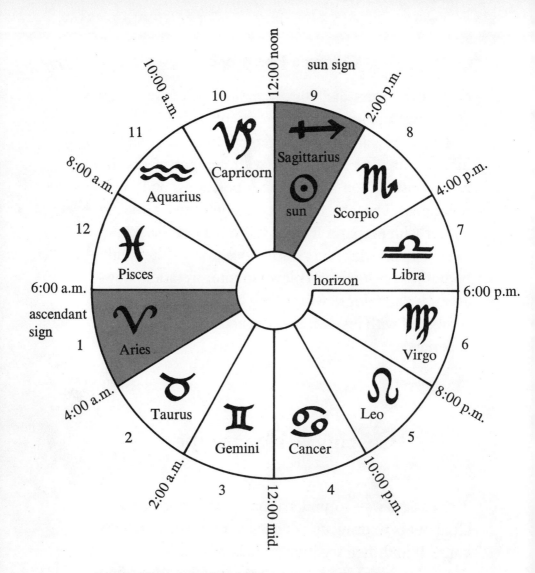

Sample birth chart showing
sun sign, ascendant sign, hour
markers, and house numbers

2. Draw a circle and divide it into twelve equal parts. Mark the line which represents the horizon as shown in the sample circular birth chart. Label the vertical line "noon" at the top and "midnight" at the bottom.

3. Starting at "noon," continue to the right around the twelve division lines, marking each at two-hour intervals:

> 2 p.m., 4 p.m., 6 p.m., 8 p.m., 10 p.m.,
>   12 Midnight
> 2 a.m., 4 a.m., 6 a.m., 8 a.m., 10 a.m.,
>   12 Noon

4. Find the section of the circle that contains the time of day you were born. Use standard time. Draw the symbol for the sun, a circle with a dot, in that section. In the same section also draw the zodiac symbol of your sun sign.

5. Working backwards, or counterclockwise, around the circle from the section containing your sun sign, draw the remaining eleven sun signs, one in each section. The diagram shows the order of the signs. If you decide you want to memorize the counterclockwise order, you can use the following nonsense couplet:

The Ramble Twins Crab Liverish;
Scaly Scorpions Are Good Water Fish.

The couplet gives clues to all of the signs as follows:

Ram	Aries the *Ram*
ble	Taurus the *Bull*
Twins	Gemini the *Twins*
Crab	Cancer the *Crab*
Li-	Leo the *Lion*
ver (ish)	Virgo the *Virgin*
Scaly	Libra the *Scales*
Scorpions	Scorpio the *Scorpion*
Are	Sagittarius the *Ar*cher
Good	Capricorn the *Go*at
Water	Aquarius the *Water* Bearer
Fish	Pisces the *Fish*

6. The sign that falls in the circle section between 4 a.m. and 6 a.m. is the sign that was rising at the horizon when you were born. This is called your ascendant.

7. The twelve circle sections also represent the houses. Number these sections from 1 to 12 counterclockwise starting from house 1, the section occupied by your ascendant sign.

Interpreting a Horoscope

You have now completed some of the first steps in drawing up your birth chart. You can look up traditional interpretations of your sun sign, your ascendant sign, and the house occupied by your sun sign at your particular time of birth. Common zodiacal sign interpretations begin on page 54. Traditional house interpretations are on page 82.

If your birth date falls nearly between two sun signs, read the interpretation for both signs. If your birth time falls exactly on one of the two-hour division lines, check the ascendants and the houses on both sides of the dividers. If you happened to be born between 4 a.m. and 6 a.m., the sun would be rising along with your sign and so your sun sign and your ascendant sign will be the same. Otherwise, read the interpretations for both your sun sign and your ascendant sign. Your horoscope will be influenced by both signs.

The professional astrologer, using an ephemeris, will map the positions of moon and planets in your chart as well. Some of the books dealing with astrology also have simplified tables that can be used. If you are interested, you may want to ask an experienced astrologer to help you.

Astrological Symbols

Here are some of the traditional ideas associated with the sun and sun signs, the moon, and the planets, their positions and angles.

THE SUN AND THE SUN SIGNS

To most of the ancients, the sun was like another planet, since it crossed the heavens along with the rest of the lights of the sky. But being the greatest light and the bringer of warmth and daytime, it was worshiped universally as the king of the gods. To the Babylonians the sun was Shamash, the bearer of life and justice. The Egyptians had three gods—Horus, Ra, and Atmu—for the rising sun, the noonday sun, and the setting sun. The Greeks called it Helios, and the Romans named it Sol. Traditionally the sun was thought to be carried across the heavens in a boat or chariot.

Modern astronomers locate the sun at the center of the solar system, which is named for it. It is a star about 860,000 miles in diameter, or ten times as wide as the giant planet Jupiter. Its radiations and emanations are necessary to life on earth and also sometimes harmful.

In astrology the sun is considered a good influence, the symbol of creative power, wisdom, dignity, generosity, and authority. Its position in the zodiac at birth is thought to be especially important and influential, determining the sign that dominates the horoscope.

⍰ ARIES

Four thousand years ago the sun was in Aries on the first day of spring. Although the relationship is no longer the same, Aries is still the sign of spring and the dates for Aries include March 21, the first day of spring when day and night are equal. The name of the sign comes from the Latin word for *ram*. The early Chaldeans sacrificed a ram at the time of spring planting in March. For both Jews and

Christians the lamb is a symbol in important festivals that occur in the spring.

Aries indicates new beginnings, the ability to start new projects and to help others with new ideas. This first sign is associated with the head, so Aries people are said to be impulsive and headstrong, characteristics also typical of the ram. Mars is said to influence or rule Aries.

TAURUS

This star constellation represents a bull, so Taurus people are said to have some of the qualities of the animal. They are inclined to be stubborn and determined but also very patient and slow to anger. At their best, Taurus people are steady and reliable, and at worst impossible to change once a decision has been made. The planet Venus rules this sign and gives the person a love of beauty, music, and art. This second sign is associated with the neck and shoulders. Therefore, the voice, in speaking or singing, may be particularly important to Taureans.

GEMINI

The constellation Gemini is seen as a set of twins, and so Gemini people are said to have "double" personalities. They have a tendency to be very changeable or, at worst, unreliable. The planet Mercury rules Gemini, adding qualities associated with the Roman messenger of the gods. Therefore, one born under Gemini may be fast-moving, agile, and flexible, able to adapt quickly to new ideas and situations. Mercury's influence is said to cause Gemini

people to be attracted to communications, perhaps with a flair for writing, acting, or an interest in transportation. Gemini people also are able to succeed at two or more occupations at once. Gemini is associated with the arms.

CANCER

Cancer is the first summer sign, beginning on June 21 and marking the longest day of the year. For this reason the early Egyptians pictured this sign as the scarab beetle, symbol of their creator sun-god, Khepera. In traditional astrology this constellation is a crab. Cancerians are thought to have the crab's

hard outer shell, making them keep to themselves. They are shy and hard to get to know, protective and secretive. The moon's rule makes Cancerians intuitive, moody, and imaginative. They may have a tendency to eat or drink a good deal, since this sign is associated with the stomach. The stomach was traditionally thought to be the source of the emotions, so there may be a tendency to be over-sensitive. Being very shy and dreamy, Cancerians are expected to be interested in mystery and the occult.

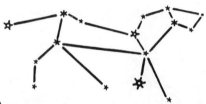

LEO

This constellation represents a lion, and people under its sign are supposed to have the characteristics associated with the king of beasts. A Leo person likes authority and tends to dominate the activities that he is involved with. He expects and demands respect. Though slow to anger, he may become en-raged when someone tries to get the better of him.

Since the sun is said to govern Leo, these people are expected to have a friendly, sunny disposition and to be warm and generous. They are also affectionate, for this sign is associated with the heart and is supposed to rule affection. A Leo is original, able to put ideas into action, and may be particularly good at directing others. He also may have a flair for the dramatic.

VIRGO

This constellation stands for that which is youthful, beautiful, and pure in both mind and body. Virgo people are expected to enjoy learning and to

take good care of themselves. They are said to seldom show their true age because of their tendency toward youthfulness. Since Mercury rules Virgo as well as Gemini, a Virgo person may show some of the characteristics associated with the messenger god—a love of communication and travel, flexibility, speed, and knowledge. Virgo people are thought to be practical, with a liking for detail and order. Along with a capacity for logic and reason goes an interest in beauty, art, and intuition.

LIBRA

Libra is seen as the scales of balance. About 4000 years ago the sun was in Libra on the first day of fall, when day and night were equal. So Libra represents everything to do with balance, harmony, and justice. Libra people dislike conflict and are natural peacemakers. They are perfectionists as well. The Libra personality is thought to stay away from extremes and to be steady and agreeable, neither overly cautious nor overly aggressive. The planet

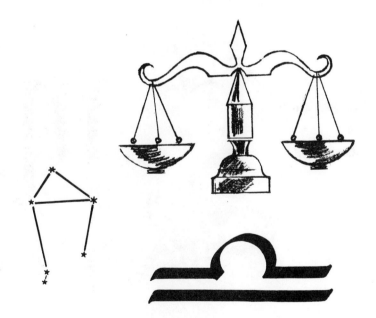

Venus is said to rule Libra, and reinforces the Libran's love of beauty, peace, and harmony. These qualities are associated with an interest in art, music, and literature. Libra governs the kidneys and lower back.

SCORPIO

Scorpio is represented by the shape of the deadly insect, the scorpion. This sign stands for shrewdness and a nature that tends to be secretive. It is associ-

ated with the reproductive organs and with powerful emotions and creative abilities. Scorpio people
are strongly attracted to members of the opposite
sex. They are believed to possess a pull toward the
lofty and spiritual combined with the aggressive evil
power of the scorpion. Scorpios are at their worst
when their emotions get the better of them and at
their best when they use their resources of strength
and energy in useful and creative directions. Scorpio
is governed by the planet Mars.

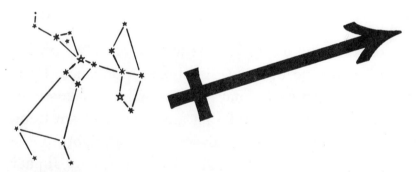

SAGITTARIUS

The archer that this constellation represents is
half man, half horse. Sagittarians are said to love
sports, freedom, and independence. Aided by the
hunter's eye, they are expected to have keen vision

or foresight and to be able to look ahead to predict the outcome of many situations in advance. However, Sagittarians may be inclined to make sharp remarks that sting like an arrow as they are frank and straightforward, always coming right to the point. Traditionally Sagittarius is ruled by Jupiter and is associated with the thighs.

CAPRICORN
Capricorn is the first winter sign, beginning on December 22 and marking the shortest day of the

year. This constellation is drawn in the shape of a sea goat, half goat and half fish. Capricorn people are expected to have the sure-footed abilities of the goat as a climber. Therefore, they should be good at meeting challenges well and rising above all sorts of obstacles. They set goals and through patience, care, and good sense of balance are able to reach them. They are serious and practical and are supposed to make good leaders. Saturn, the planet of discipline and constriction, rules Capricorn, and attention to discipline is the secret of success for one born under the sign. Since Capricorn is associated

with the knees, use of the legs may be important, but physical problems may arise in this area.

AQUARIUS

Aquarius is the water-bearer. In early times, the constellation was seen as a water pitcher. The Greeks showed it as a man, Ganymede, the cup-bearer of the gods. Since water is the sustaining element, and flowing water represents the life force, this constellation is associated with truth, or the source of life and knowledge. Representing an in-

terest in all life everywhere, it has become the humanitarian symbol, and Aquarians are expected to be concerned about equality and brotherhood. Other traditional characteristics are generosity and a love of art and the mystic. Aquarius is thought to be an especially creative sign and to be ruled by Uranus, god of the heavens. The calves and the ankles are assigned to Aquarius.

In 1962, the planets visible to the naked eye all appeared in near conjunction in this sign. Some astrologers feel that this occurrence may have signaled the birth of an influential world leader. The sun now is entering the constellation on the first day of spring, so we are beginning "the age of Aquarius."

PISCES

This sign is depicted as two fish on the end of a double line. Immersed in the all-encompassing sea, Pisceans are supposed to be interested in unity and that which lies beneath the surface. Thus, they may

be drawn to the mystic or occult. They are thought of as somewhat timid, like meandering fish, and inclined to "drift with the tide." Pisceans may be too gullible for their own good. On the other hand, they may be able to put intuition and psychic abilities to good use. Being associated with water gives Pisceans a fluid nature. The brightest star of Pisces is Al Risha. Several years before Christ's birth, the planets Mars, Jupiter, and Saturn appeared in near conjunction with this bright star. This combination could have been the "bright star" associated with the birth of Jesus. In any case, the fish always has been an important symbol in Christianity, and the symbolism doubtless has added to the idea that Pisceans may have strong religious feelings. Pisces governs the feet, another reason for considering it the ruler of that which is below, or hidden. Because the sun appeared in Pisces on the first day of spring for the last 2000 years, that period was considered the "age of the fish."

THE MOON

Appearing about the same size as the sun when it is full, the earth's moon was given almost equal importance by the ancients. It is about 2160 miles in diameter, large enough so that astronomers sometimes consider the earth and its moon as a double planet system. Being the brightest light in the night sky when it is visible, it was associated with dreams and intuition. To the Babylonians the moon was the god Sin, who drove out darkness and controlled dreams and prophecy. The Greeks changed it to the goddess Selene, who was later called Artemis, goddess of the hunt and protector of women. To the Romans it became Diana.

Traditionally the moon has been associated with change and with femininity, and its phases were thought to influence moods and fertility. The full moon also has been associated with insanity, hence the common word *lunacy*, from the Latin word for moon, *luna*. Along with the sun, the moon controls the tides.

Astrologers believe the moon to be as important as the sun in its position in the zodiac at birth. It is considered a flexible influence, symbol of femininity, imagination, emotion, and intuition.

THE PLANETS

Because of their movements, their color, or their association with gods and goddesses, the planets are believed to have special astrological influences.

MERCURY

Mercury is the nearest planet to the sun. Although it is only 3000 miles in diameter, less than half that of the earth, it can be seen with the naked eye. Its orbit is close to the sun, and it appears to move quickly against the background of stars, circling the sun once every eighty-eight days. It is named for the fleet-footed Roman messenger of the gods who presided over communications, travel, commerce, science, and eloquence. To the ancient Babylonians the planet was associated with the god Nebo, the announcer, who recorded the deeds of men and was the patron of wisdom, learning, and writing. The Greeks assigned it to Hermes, god of science, eloquence, and cunning.

Borrowing from these associations, modern astrology considers Mercury the planet of science, intelligence, learning, communication, travel, and business.

VENUS

According to ancient legend, Venus was born out of the head of Jupiter. A few astronomers have suggested that there may be a factual basis to this myth. One theory of the solar system postulated that Venus was originally a comet, perhaps even formed of material thrown off from Jupiter, before falling into its present orbit. Some feel that its rotation, which is opposite that of the other planets, the dense composition of its present atmosphere, and its very high temperature support this view.

Venus orbits the sun between the earth and Mercury. It is 7522 miles in diameter, only slightly

smaller than the earth. Partly because of its heavy
cloud cover, Venus looks whitish to the naked eye.
It is the brightest feature of the night sky, next to
the moon. Because its orbit is also near the sun,
Venus is sometimes not visible at all during the
night. At times it appears as the "morning star" and
at other times as the "evening star," in each case being seen low over the horizon.

Venus is named for the Roman goddess of spring,
love, and beauty. The Greeks also called the planet
Phosphor, the light bearer, because of its color and
brightness. To the ancient Babylonians the planet
was Ishtar, the goddess of earth, love, and marriage.

Modern astrologers consider Venus the planet
ruling love, beauty, marriage, gentleness, intuition,
and creativity, inducing a love of music and art.

MARS

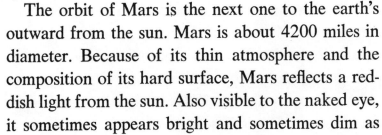

The orbit of Mars is the next one to the earth's
outward from the sun. Mars is about 4200 miles in
diameter. Because of its thin atmosphere and the
composition of its hard surface, Mars reflects a reddish light from the sun. Also visible to the naked eye,
it sometimes appears bright and sometimes dim as

the orbits of earth and Mars bring the planets closer together or farther apart. Its fiery appearance earned it an association with war and violence. Among the Babylonians, it was Nergal, god of war and death. The Greeks called it Ares, and later the Romans gave it the name of their war god, Mars.

Mars always had been linked with catastrophe: wars, earthquakes, volcanoes, and the like. A few historians suggest that once Mars may have had a different orbit in which it approached the earth more closely. There are numerous myths of attacks by this planet god, resulting in great upheavals on the earth. Some early records show knowledge of the existence of Mars's two small moons, which are not visible today without use of a telescope.

Traditionally astrologers have associated Mars with military careers, courage, strength, an aggressive nature, and a quick temper.

JUPITER

Jupiter is the largest of the planets. It is about 86,700 miles in diameter or more than ten times the diameter of the earth. It is almost large enough to be a star and is a strong source of radiation, in addition to reflecting light from the sun. Jupiter is visible to the naked eye and moves slowly, taking almost twelve years to orbit the sun as it appears to move once around the zodiac.

The ancient Babylonians called Jupiter Marduk, after their fierce creator god of lightning and thunder. The Greeks called the planet Zeus, ascribing to it the qualities of their powerful creator who was thought to be noble and generous and a bringer of wealth and good fortune. Today we use the name of the Roman king of the gods, Jupiter.

Modern astrologers believe people born under Jupiter will tend to be strong, healthy, and endowed with long life and good fortune.

SATURN

Saturn is the second largest planet, being about 72,400 miles in diameter. It is the next planet beyond Jupiter and orbits the sun once every twenty-nine and a half years. Saturn is visible to the naked eye and appears slightly yellowish as it moves very slowly along the background of fixed stars. Only through the telescope are its rings visible.

The Babylonians called the planet Ninib, after
their god of evil influence. To the Greeks it was
Cronus, ruler of the universe and god of the harvest.
The Romans gave the planet the name Saturn after
their god of planting and the harvest.

In modern astrology Saturn is a planet of mixed
influence. It is associated with discipline, control,
and setting limits, so that it is referred to as "the
taskmaster."

URANUS

The planet Uranus, which is 29,200 miles in diameter, cannot be seen with the naked eye. It was
discovered by an amateur astronomer, Sir William
Herschel, in 1781. Herschel named it for King
George III of England, but at first it was called
after him instead, and it still carries the symbol,
H. Later the name was changed to Uranus after
the Greek god of the heavens. The rotational axis
of Uranus is tilted so much that, compared with
the rest of the planets, it is somewhat like a top
spinning on its side. Being the seventh planet out
from the sun, it takes eighty-four earth years to
make one orbit around it.

Since its discovery, Uranus has acquired a host of associations. It is considered new and strange, perhaps because of the tilt of its axis, and is said to trigger sudden and unexpected occurrences, such as earthquakes. It is believed to induce events that are revolutionary and visionary, possibly of a humanitarian nature. People influenced by Uranus can be expected to be eccentric, inventive, and progressive. Uranus rules Aquarius.

NEPTUNE

The eighth planet is Neptune, discovered by the German astronomer, Johann Gottfried Galle, in 1846. About 28,200 miles in diameter, Neptune takes approximately 164 earth years to go once around the sun.

Neptune was named for the Roman god of the sea, and so astrologers have associated it with the constellation Pisces. The planet, therefore, is thought to have some of the same connotations as the constellation of the fish. Neptune is said to rule the religious, mystical, and psychic, and those influenced by this planet also are said to be changeable in nature and to be attracted to the sea.

PLUTO

As a result of predictions made by the American astronomer Percival Lowell, Pluto was discovered in 1930 by another American astronomer, Clyde Tombaugh. The name, that of the Greek god of the underworld, conveniently contains the initials of Percival Lowell in its first two letters, *P* and *L*, and the first two letters of Clyde Tombaugh's last name in its last two letters, *T* and *O*.

Pluto is so far from the sun that there is not yet complete agreement on its diameter. It has an off-center and tilted orbit compared with that of the other planets, and astronomers theorize that it may be either a moon escaped from Neptune or perhaps a large comet captured by the solar system.

Pluto takes about thirteen years to move through just one sign of the zodiac. Since its discovery has been so recent, astrologers have not come to any agreement on its symbolic influence. Many do not include it in horoscope interpretation.

THE HOUSES

Just as the zodiac is divided into twelve constellations, so the same twelve-part division is used to designate the so-called houses. The thirty-degree sections of sky that rise above the horizon at two-hour intervals, the houses are numbered starting at the horizon at the time of a person's birth. Probably the idea of individual sectional time markers began with the early Egyptians, who referred to "places," but it was Manilius, the Roman astrologer, who first popularized the concept of houses.

The first house is the section occupied by the ascendant sign at the moment of birth. The remaining houses are numbered backward around the circular birth chart in the order that they will appear above the horizon.

The relationship of the houses is based on the perfect triangle, a sacred symbol in religion and astrology from ancient times. If one draws such an equal-sided triangle within the circle starting with one of the circumference points of house number 1, the other two points of the triangle will touch houses 5 and 9. These three houses are said to be *individual* and relate to the self, which includes man's body, emotions, and spirit. A second triangle that starts with house number 2 will touch houses 6 and 10. These houses are designated *temporal*

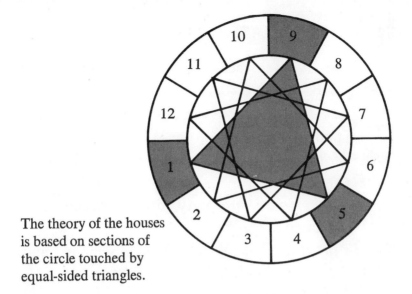

The theory of the houses is based on sections of the circle touched by equal-sided triangles.

and influence man's possessions, comforts, and honors. The third triangle that starts with house number 3 will touch houses 7 and 11 and is said to be *relative*. These houses govern man's relationships to others in the form of family, travel, marriage and partnership, and friendships. A last triangle starts with house number 4 and touches houses 8 and 12. It is called *terminal*. These houses concern endings: man's final condition, death, and limitations.

Following this scheme, the houses have these common interpretations:

First House: personality, appearance, and disposition

Second House: possessions, money, and appetites

Third House: sisters, brothers, other relatives, and short trips

Fourth House: property, home, parents, and security

Fifth House: love affairs, amusements and pleasures, and children

Sixth House: health, physical comforts, and employees or servants

Seventh House: partnerships, contracts, and marriage

Eighth House: death, losses, and wills

Ninth House: wisdom, religion, intuition, and extended travel

Tenth House: occupation, fame, and honors

Eleventh House: friends, associates, social contacts, and wishes

Twelfth House: restrictions, confinement, limitations, and weaknesses

Thus, when an astronomer knows which planet was in which house at the time of birth, he feels that he can determine what influences will affect the various aspects of life.

POSITIVE AND NEGATIVE SIGNS

According to tradition, the twelve signs of the zodiac are alternately positive or negative. The first sign, Aries, is designated positive; Taurus is negative, Gemini positive, Cancer negative, Leo positive, Virgo negative, Libra positive, Scorpio negative, Sagittarius positive, Capricorn negative, Aquarius positive, and Pisces negative.

Some astrologers interpret these designations to mean that characteristics generally considered masculine are stressed in some signs, while those considered feminine are stressed in others. A more recent idea is that people born under a positive sign are "electric." They move out to acquire what they want and need. Those born under a negative sign are "magnetic." They tend to attract what they want and need.

THE ELEMENTS

The ancients believed that the four original elements were earth, air, fire, and water. A relation-

ship between these four elements and the twelve
signs of the zodiac was established on the basis
of the equal-sided triangle. Aries is a fire sign. Laid
out on the zodiacal chart, a perfect triangle with
Aries at one corner touches Leo and Saggitarius,
also considered fire signs. Continuing the triangle
pattern around the zodiac, Taurus, Virgo, and
Capricorn are considered earth signs. Gemini,
Libra, and Aquarius are air signs. And finally,
Cancer, Scorpio, and Pisces are water signs. Although Aquarius turns out to be an air sign, as
the water-bearer it also symbolizes water. The fire
signs and air signs are considered masculine, while
earth and water are feminine.

Some astrologers further divide each zodiacal sign
into three ten-degree sections called "decanates."
According to this system, if your birth date falls
within the first decanate of your sun sign, the influence of the sun sign will be very strong. If your
birth date falls in the second decanate, you also
will be strongly influenced by the next sign, counterclockwise, that shares your element. Born in the
third decanate, you will feel the influence of the
remaining sign assigned to your element.

THE ASPECTS

The term *aspects* refers to the angles between the sun, moon, or planets and the earth, as they occur in the zodiac at a particular time. There are six important angles, four of them considered usually favorable, while two are considered unfavorable.

1. *Conjunction:* Two planets on the same side of the earth and nearly aligned with it form no angle with the earth and are said to be in conjunction. On the chart the planets are in the same sign and also are in conjunction. This position is usually considered a favorable influence, depending on the particular planets involved.

2. *Trine:* Planets forming an angle of 120 degrees with the earth establish two points of a perfect triangle on the chart and are said to be in trine. This angle is considered the most favorable of all aspects. Signs that are four signs, or 120 degrees, apart from each other on the chart also are in the trine relationship.

3. *Sextile:* Planets forming an angle of 60 degrees with the earth and signs that are 60 degrees apart on the chart are in sextile. This angle is a

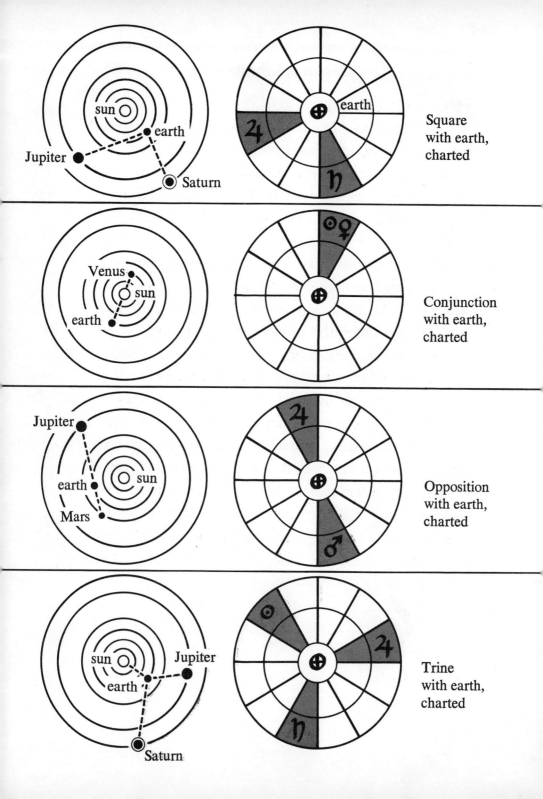

Square
with earth,
charted

Conjunction
with earth,
charted

Opposition
with earth,
charted

Trine
with earth,
charted

subdivision of the trine and considered favorable.

4. *Semisextile:* Planets forming an angle of 30 degrees with the earth and signs that are neighbors on the chart are in semisextile. This angle is considered somewhat favorable.

5. *Opposition:* Planets on nearly opposite sides of the earth (or six signs apart on the chart) form a 180-degree angle with the earth and are said to be in opposition. This angle is usually considered unfavorable.

6. *Square:* Planets forming an angle of 90 degrees, or a square corner with the earth, and signs that are 90 degrees apart on the chart are said to be in square. This angle is considered an unfavorable relationship.

Astrologers differ on interpreting angles that are close but not exact. Some feel that a conjunction or opposition must be within one or two degrees to be considered, allowing about five degrees for other aspects. Other astrologers allow approximations within eight to ten degrees of the correct angle for all aspects.

Astrologers not only compute birth charts and

horoscopes for individuals but for organizations, countries, and world events as well. In these cases, the date of the founding of an organization or a new government is used for the predictions. And for individuals who are interested in keeping up-to-date with themselves, astrologers will prepare progressed horoscopes. These charts may be figured at any time after the original horoscope. The astrologer notes the positions of the heavenly bodies on the anniversary of the birthday or at the special time requested and compares them with those on the original birth chart. There is no end to the ways the sky can be "read" for signs affecting the fate of men and nations.

Still, it is important to remember that for all of the evidence suggesting that traditional astrology is valid, there is at least as much evidence that it is not. For instance, French mathematician Michel Gauquelin used a simple experiment to test the effect of a horoscope on the person receiving it. To a group of people, each of whom requested an individual horoscope, he gave a chart that was complete but false, having nothing to do with the actual positions of the heavenly bodies at the time of birth.

The character analysis was the same for every person. In response to these fake horoscopes, Gauquelin received many letters praising him for his ability to analyze character and give advice. This response does not mean that there may not be some value to traditional astrology. But it does suggest that much of the success of astrology may depend on the astrologer's own intuition and ability to give good general advice to many people.

III
Scientific Astrology

In recent decades, with the need to discover how to make space travel safe, scientists have studied the ways in which human beings are affected by electromagnetic fields and cosmic radiations. Some pioneer researchers have found new evidence of the effects of the positions and motions of sun, moon, and planets on earth's life. Studies of solar and other cosmic radiations have shown that man is extremely susceptible to changes in their distribution and strength.

The new findings point to principles remarkably similar to a few of the ideas of traditional astrology. Perhaps behind the superstition and exaggeration of these ancient beliefs is a core of factual knowledge, which was at one time understood and applied. To a certain extent, the new discoveries may be rediscoveries of knowledge that had been partly lost. But whether the ideas are old or new, the modern pioneers, using the tools and measurements of twentieth-century technology, are bringing us a better understanding of man's relationship to the cosmos.

The Moon

The ancient Babylonians believed that the moon influenced both the weather and fertility. Recently the Egyptologist, Dr. Barna Balogh, rediscovered an early Babylonian weather rule stating that the weather can change completely only five days after a new or full moon. And whatever weather develops on such a key day will prevail for the next two weeks. Balogh, a Hungarian, decided to check weather records in his country to see if there was any evidence of such a correlation. According to Dr. Balogh, the general rule does work to a surprising degree.

In the United States, Glenn Brier of the United States Weather Bureau in Washington reported on rainfall surveys over a period of fifty years. There was a significant tendency for the heaviest twenty-four-hour rains to come about three to five days after full moon and new moon in North America. Another meteorologist, D. A. Bradley, found that more hurricanes began at new and full moon.

Do the moon's phases also affect people? The belief that the full moon triggered insanity produced our word *lunatic*. Modern studies show that there may be evidence to suport this idea. According to the Philadelphia Police Department, the crime rate goes up during periods of full moon, particularly those called "mad" crimes. Dr. R. D. J. Ravitz, of the University of Pennsylvania School of Medicine, conducted an experiment with a group of people in good mental health. By means of electrodes, the differences in positive and negative electrical potential in each person were measured. The greatest differences came at times of new and full moon. Tests with mentally ill patients at Duke Hospital in Virginia showed similar results, but with the disturbed patients the results were more exaggerated. With both groups new and full moon caused changes in mood.

At full moon the number of positive ions in the atmosphere increases, while more negative ions are produced when the moon wanes. Experiments show that human beings tend to be stimulated by negative ions and depressed by positive ions. In hospitals negative ions have been used to assist in speeding the healing of wounds and to help patients feel more cheerful.

Apparently the clotting of blood also is affected. A Florida medical doctor, Edson Andrews, who kept records of 1000 patients over a three-year period, found that four out of five cases of severe bleeding occurred between the moon's first and third quarters or during the period of full moon.

The full moon has been found to stimulate births among expectant mothers. According to the late Dr. Eldon Tice, of Los Angeles Methodist Hospital, more babies are born each month during the forty-eight-hour full-moon period. Furthermore, a woman's body rhythm long has been thought to be related to the phases of the moon. While the physical cycles of most women do not match the moon's phases over an extended period, still on an average of twenty-eight days a woman's body produces a

moon

earth

sun

Researchers report that at full moon there are more positive ions in the atmosphere, the body's electrical balance changes, there are more crimes, more cases of severe bleeding, and more babies born.

tiny egg and prepares itself for carrying a child. This twenty-eight-day period is only a rough average, but it is quite close to the length of several of the moon's periodic cycles of motion.

In the 1950's, a psychiatrist in Czechoslovakia began putting together some ideas that were to lead to remarkable theories about the moon and the timing of the start of human life. Dr. Eugen Jonas was a student of astrology. He had watched the changing behavior of hospital patients, which seemed at times to follow phases of the moon. Dr. Jonas also was intrigued with the Babylonian idea that the phases of the moon controlled a woman's fertility—the time when a new baby could be conceived.

Studying many case histories of pregnancy and birth timing, Dr. Jonas decided that certain patterns could be seen. Apparently a grown woman was regularly fertile during the same moon phase that had occurred at the time of her own birth. Dr. Jonas found a second pattern that related to another old astrological idea. It was that the traditional designations of positive or negative to each sign in the zodiac seemed to have something to do with the birth of boys or girls, but in a way no one had thought of before.

Taking birth records and estimating the month when conception occurred—when the new baby first began growing in the mother—Dr. Jonas found that when conception occurred while the moon was in a positive sign of the zodiac at the time of the mother's fertile moon phase, there was an 85 percent chance the baby would be a boy. If conception occurred when the moon was crossing through a negative sign of the zodiac, the baby was likely to be a girl.

These conclusions seemed almost impossible to

believe, so Jonas set out to test both findings with women who were planning their families. Sixty couples were chosen who did not wish to have any more children. Dr. Jonas made a chart for each woman for a year showing, according to the moon phase, when each woman was fertile and when she was not. The couples were to avoid mating during the days marked as fertile by Dr. Jonas. At the end of the test year this system of birth-control timing proved to have been 96 percent successful.

Meanwhile, tests with other couples who were trying to have a child of a particular sex showed equally promising results. For example, couples who already had three or four girls in a row were able to have a boy when the wife conceived during the moon-position timing plotted by Dr. Jonas.

The Astra-Nitra clinic was set up in Czecho-slovakia to compute charts for women wanting to use the Jonas system. In late 1970, the Astra Scientific Board reported that of 1252 women who had used the birth-control charts for a year, 1224 had been successful, an average of 97.7 percent. Later Astra International was begun in Vienna, Austria, to handle additional requests. It is estimated that

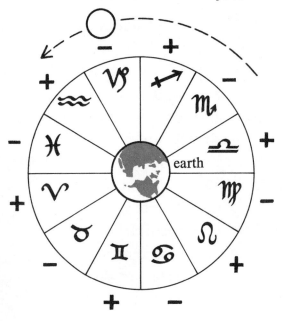

Moon takes about 2½ days in each 30° section.

Astrologers consider the zodiacal signs alternately positive and negative. According to Dr. Eugen Jonas, boy babies are conceived when the moon is in a positive sign and girls when the moon is in a negative sign.

over 40,000 women have had charts drawn up. Doctors using the system report a continued high percentage of success.

Besides the statistics from these experiments, is there other scientific evidence to support Dr. Jonas's methods? Three Soviet scientists—Kolstov, Schroder, and Asztanrov—were able to separate male-producing and female-producing sperm using electrical charges. It is known that sperm from a male animal carry genes that unite with other genes in the tiny egg of the female animal. Those sperm that produce females carry an extra gene. They are called X sperm, while the others are designated Y sperm. The Soviet scientists found that if positive and negative electrical poles are set up, the Y sperm can be attracted by the negative pole while the X sperm can be attracted by the positive pole. This and other research involving electrical polarities give us some reason to believe that a scientific basis to Dr. Jonas's system may be found, but too little is known at this time.

If Dr. Jonas's work is correct, every woman actually has two fertility cycles instead of one. A woman's body, of course, produces an egg about once every twenty-eight days, following a cycle determined by its present biological rhythm. At times this fertility cycle may overlap with the one established by the moon phase at her birth. At other times these two cycles may be quite separate. Doctors who have developed the Jonas system further now use charts including both cycles, and they claim excellent results.

The Sun

The sun is the energy giver and regulator of life on earth. Or more correctly, it is the earth-sun system that sets the patterns. There is the cycle of earth's daily rotation, the cycle of the seasons, and the sun itself rotates and has its own cycles of activity. As discoveries have been made in chemistry and physics, the ways in which the sun is known to affect our lives have multiplied. A vast array of waves and particles from the sun strike the earth and are absorbed by living things or by particles in the atmosphere. At times magnetic storms on the sun increase this bombardment of particles, and surprisingly even the planets themselves seem to have something to do with changes on the sun and on the earth as well.

DAILY CYCLE

As the earth rotates once each twenty-four hours its atmosphere, land, and water are heated by the sun's radiant energy, and they are allowed to cool as they turn away from the sun. Sunlight not only brings warmth, but the pattern of light and dark governs the activity of many inhabitants of the planet. Daylight animals are stimulated by the sunrise, and nocturnal animals are stimulated by darkness. We tend to take these patterns for granted without realizing how completely our lives are regulated by day and night.

The earth's rotation also causes effects that are not so well known but just as regular as the cycle of activity and rest. According to ancient Chinese belief, the organs of the body are most active at particular times of the twenty-four-hour period, maintaining a regular daily schedule. Doctors today have become aware of some of these cycles. For instance, a hospital watches patients with a liver ailment closely during the hours of 11:00 P.M to 1:00 A.M. At that time the liver tends to become most active and more problems may arise with it. Obstetricians know that more expectant mothers begin labor around midnight than at any other time and that more babies are born in the early-morning hours. Furthermore, each of us has his own twenty-four-hour temperature cycle, with high and low points that stay regular day after day.

YEARLY CYCLE

Since the earth tilts on its axis about 23 degrees from the vertical, a seasonal pattern occurs over most of the globe as the earth orbits around the sun once in about 365 days. The seasons regulate earth life, stimulating periods of growth and fertility and periods of dormancy and hibernation. The length of the day gradually changes from short to long and back again, and we change our activities with this cycle.

The tilt of the earth also produces further effects. In the northern hemisphere more children are born in the summer months, and these children are heavier on the average than those born at other times of the year. In the southern hemisphere, where the timing of the seasons is reversed, the birth statistics also are reversed.

Because of the earth's tilt, the apparent angle of the sun's path in the sky gradually changes. The highest angle in the northern hemisphere produces the longest stretch of daylight hours and falls on about June 21. Then the angle gradually decreases until the low point, which produces the shortest day, comes around December 22.

The fluctuation of the sun's angle is like the swinging of a pendulum, creating stresses that affect the earth in several ways. Often these change points, called the solstices, are accompanied by periods of unusual weather, with more storms than usual. For example, tropical storm Agnes, which caused severe flooding along parts of the east coast of the United States in 1972, came exactly at the time of the summer solstice.

Observers have reported that the sun's reversal in altitude at the solstices seems to cause internal strains in mountain ranges. The earth-moon-sun lineups that follow the solstices cause additional strains because of the tidal effect on the earth, creating likely situations for earthquakes.

SUNSPOT CYCLE

It has been known for hundreds of years that there are sometimes spots, or splotches, on the face of the sun. An ancient Chinese stargazer described them as "flying birds upon the sun." Occasionally some of the larger spots are visible even without a telescope because of their great size. A sunspot may last anywhere from several days to several months.

Often sunspots appear in pairs. Scientists believe them to be enormous magnetic storms on the sun.

One man who made an important study of these unusual spots was a physician living in Nice, France. Dr. Maurice Faure noticed that on certain days the telephone service was disturbed for no apparent reason. No lines were down, and the electrical machinery was in working order, but connections would go dead or be made inaccurately. Then, just as strangely, everything would return to normal. Dr. Faure noticed that these interruptions in the phone service seemed to match outbreaks of illness. More people became ill when the service was bad and fewer people when the telephones were normal. He felt that there must be some factor causing these things to happen at the same time.

The newspapers carried a story about a magnetic storm in the United States that had interrupted telephone communication there for several hours. Dr. Faure contacted M. Vallot, a French astronomer, who told him that sunspots might be the cause of such storms. The two men, along with another physician, Dr. Sardou, decided to test the theory. Over a period of 267 days the astronomer noted the

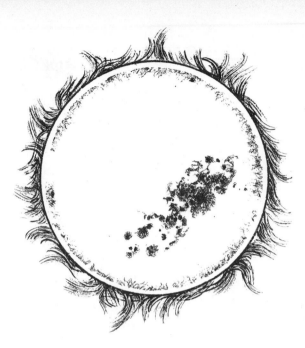

Drawing from a
photograph of dense
sunspot clusters
seen during period
of high activity

movement of sunspots across the rotating surface
of the sun. Dr. Sardou kept health records daily at
Nice on the Mediterranean shore, and Dr. Faure
kept a similar count of illnesses at Lamalou, in
central France. The three men did not compare
notes until the end of the test period, when they
found the times of increasing illness were alike in
both locations and seemed to match periods of high
sunspot activity. The results of their study were published in 1922.

About the same time A. L. Tchijewski, of the

University of Moscow, was gathering related statistics. Being an historian, he wanted to find out if
there were patterns in the appearance of world
events such as wars and plagues. Tchijewski made
a survey of recurring social events running from
500 B.C. to 1900 A.D., the turn of the twentieth century. He decided to compare the tabulations of
world events with sunspot activity, which had been
found to increase regularly in an extended cycle at
intervals of eleven and one-tenth years.

Tchijewski believed he found correlations between human cycles and the eleven-year sunspot
cycle. For example, he noticed that over a period of
one hundred years the changes of government in
England seemed to follow the sunspot cycle. Lib-
erals came to power during periods of high sunspot
activity, while Conservatives were in power in
years of low sunspot activity. Checking the timing
of history's great epidemics—the plagues, diphtheria,
cholera, and typhus—Tchijewski found that they
tended to occur at times of high sunspot activity. A
particularly close correlation can be seen in the
series of smallpox epidemics in Chicago before the
development of vaccines.

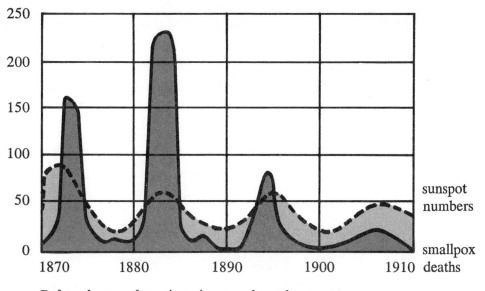

250

200

150

100

50

0

1870   1880   1890   1900   1910

sunspot
numbers

smallpox
deaths

Before the use of vaccines, increased number
of deaths during smallpox epidemics tended to
parallel peaks of sunspot activity.

While Tchijewski may have exaggerated the importance of the sunspot cycle, his pioneering work
did establish many statistical correlations. More
recent studies show that sunspot highs do affect life,
from the increase in rabbit population to the growth
of trees as seen in tree rings.

Some of the most exciting research is in basic
human chemistry. In the 1930's, hospitals in many
countries were using a blood-reaction test devel-

oped by Dr. Miki Takata, a physician at Toho University in Japan. A chemical added to blood samples causes flocculation—the formation of small lumps. The amount of flocculation, or the index, stayed the same for men but varied with women during the menstrual period. But suddenly, in January of 1938, the flocculation index began to increase in all the samples in every hospital using the test. Even the index for men began to rise in a strange way. The normal tests were no longer useful, and Takata decided there must be some outside cause, since the changes took place all over the world.

It was found that 1938 was a peak sunspot year. Keeping records over a period of twenty years, Takata discovered that the variations coincided with the activity of the sun. When groups of sunspots cross the midline of the sun, the flocculation index rises, while during low sunspot activity the index is also low. In addition, the flocculation index followed a daily curve with the rising of the sun, always increasing just a few minutes before sunrise.

Other researchers also have produced evidence that the sun affects human blood. In 1960, Soviet hematologist Nicolas Schulz reported that during high sunspot activity, particularly in the 1957 to 1958 period, the numbers of white blood cells increased. Such studies suggest that sunspot activity may be one factor contributing to a disease like leukemia, in which there are too many white blood cells and too few red cells.

In Italy, a chemist named Giorgio Piccardi was puzzled by the behavior of water in chemical experiments. For some unexplained reason there were day-to-day variations in the rates at which different materials dissolved into solution, although everything else in the experiments was the same. Piccardi first thought that there might be some correlation with changes in the weather. This theory did not prove to be valid, so he tried shielding his chemicals with metal screens. The screened chemicals did not vary in their reactions the way the unshielded ones did.

Piccardi found that several things affected the rate at which the chemicals dissolved. First, whenever there were sudden solar eruptions or storms, the reactions in the exposed test tubes were subject to violent change. At the same time the reactions in the screened test tubes remained almost entirely stable. When tests had been made for a number of years, evidence accumulated that there was also an eleven-year variation. This pattern of change matched the sunspot cycle. And finally there was a yearly variation. Reactions tended to speed up in March; abnormal changes occurred in September. Clearly the sun was causing the random variations and also the eleven-year cycle, but what was responsible for the twice-yearly changes?

Piccardi finally concluded that the cause was the earth's motion through space. The entire solar system is moving across the spiral galaxy of stars of which it is a part and the earth's orbit around the sun gives it a corkscrew motion as it moves. In March, the earth speeds through the galaxy at twenty-nine miles per second. In September its overall speed is only fourteen miles per second.

One of the most important discoveries coming from the experiments of Piccardi and Takata is that the disruptions noted all have something to do with water. Water is a part of most chemical changes, and the largest part of the human body is water. The experiments show that water is extremely susceptible to cosmic influences from beyond the earth, particularly those of the sun. And the changes in human blood chemistry show similar reactions. Apparently living beings are far more sensitive to space conditions than we had imagined, and the study of water may tell us why.

The Planets

Ever since the discovery of the sunspot pattern, scientists have tried to find a relationship between the sunspot cycle, which lasts eleven and one-tenth years, and planetary cycles. The nearest match seemed to be with the period of Jupiter, which takes just eleven and eight-tenths years to go once around the sun. Of all the planets, Jupiter has the strongest gravitational effect on the sun. But there seemed much more to the puzzle than this connection.

MAGNETIC STORMS

Scientists knew that sunspots caused magnetic storms on earth and interrupted radio communications, but interruptions occurred at other times that did not correspond with the solar flares. In 1948, J. H. Nelson, a radio propagation analyst for RCA, began to look for a possible relationship between planetary positions and radio communications. Over several years he tabulated the periods of interrupted communications and discovered that indeed there was some relationship.

Whenever two or more planets were lined up in conjunction with the sun on the same side of the sun, or were lined up in opposition on opposite sides of the sun, or formed a square, 90-degree angle with the sun, radio communication tended to be difficult. On the other hand, the best periods of clear communication seemed to be when several planets formed 120-degree angles with the sun. The large planets, Saturn and Jupiter, seemed especially important. Conjunctions, oppositions, or squares of these two planets created the worst interference, while a 120-degree angle between the same two large planets and the sun was the most stable arrangement. Similar results were observed with the smaller planets.

Calculating planetary positions in advance, RCA

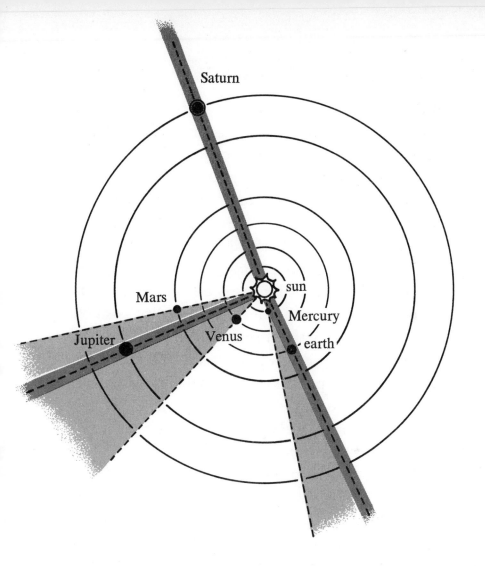

Planet positions during radio disturbances
on July 27, 1946. Saturn and Jupiter
form near 90° square with sun; Saturn
and earth in near opposition with sun.

was able to predict periods of high radio interference and, by changing broadcast frequencies at such times, to improve communications. This analysis of planetary angles has come to be called "gravitational vectoring." Not only has it helped radio communications, it has been a boon to the space program as well. Dr. Richard Head, of NASA, confirms that solar flares can be predicted from planetary angles. When solar flares do occur, they tend to be associated with the same planetary positions that cause magnetic storms on earth. Thus, the advance plotting of favorable planetary angles can help to identify periods of quiet solar activity. Since solar flares release radiation that is extremely dangerous to space travelers away from the protection of earth's atmosphere, such flights as those to the surface of the moon need to be planned during periods of quiet sun activity.

The favorable and unfavorable planetary angles of Nelson's system are much the same as those used in traditional astrology except that they are measured in relation to the sun rather than the earth. They are the angles struggled with by Kepler, who believed them to exert a real influence on the weather and earth events. Evidently this idea is one element of the old beliefs that has been found to have some basis in fact.

EARTHQUAKES

In 1953, Dr. Rudolf Tomaschek, geophysicist at the University of Munich, made a study of 134 severe earthquakes. He found that at the times and places of most of these earthquakes, the planet Uranus was close to an overhead position in the sky. During the period from 1903 to 1906, there were about four times the usual number of earthquakes. Tomaschek noted that at this time the two slowest-moving planets, Neptune and Pluto, were lined up on the opposite side of the sun from Uranus. Somehow the three-planet opposition created patterns of stress in the earth that caused quakes at places moving into line with them.

Predicting earthquakes, volcanoes, or other natural disasters according to planetary positions is not new. People had observed that many earthquakes or eruptions closely followed eclipses of the sun or moon or happened later at places where the line of an eclipse shadow had passed. Like the lineups noted by Tomaschek, eclipses are caused by exact conjunctions of heavenly bodies with the earth. For example, in a solar eclipse, the moon swings into position exactly between sun and earth so that all three form a straight line.

In 1932, an unusual oncoming conjunction came to the attention of meteorologist George McCormack. A solar eclipse was to occur on August 31. At the same time that the sun and moon were lined up on one side of the earth, the large planets Neptune and Jupiter also would come close to lining up with the sun and moon on the same side of the earth, making a near conjunction of four bodies of the solar system with the earth.

McCormack was aware that sometimes earthquake activity did not occur along the eclipse path until many weeks later. When it did take place, one of the faster-moving planets seemed to act as a trigger. Only when one of these planets moved into the place where the conjunction had earlier been would the earthquake occur. It was as if a charged gravitational or magnetic line had been set up in space at the time of the eclipse conjunction, something like the spoke of a bicycle wheel hanging in space. When a planet close to earth moved around to touch the "spoke," the charge was released.

McCormack noted that the sun-moon-Neptune-Jupiter conjunction would occur at a precise position in the constellation Leo on August 31, 1932. Between March 8 and 12, 1933, the planet Mars would be moving very close to this same section of the heavens, and on March 10 the moon also would be close to the same line.

McCormack chose March 10 as the most likely date and published his notes on the planetary alignments in "Astro Weather Guide." The August eclipse had reached totality directly over Los Angeles, California, so McCormack felt that the predicted earthquake was likely to affect this area. On March 10, both Mars and the moon moved to within two degrees of the earlier eclipse line. The slow-moving Neptune was still in almost the same position as it had been during the eclipse, so Mars, the moon, and Neptune all created a new conjunction in the same area. At 5:54 p.m. a violent earthquake struck Long Beach, California, in the predicted area, killing more than 100 people, injuring perhaps 1000, and causing millions of dollars' worth of damage. In this case, the earthquake prediction had been all too accurate.

HEREDITY

In the 1950's, Michel Gauquelin found an interesting correlation between births, planetary positions, and occupations. A survey had been made of the birth times and locations of 576 famous members of the French Academy of Medicine. Using astronomical charts of planetary positions, Gauquelin found that a large number of the famous physicians had been born when either Mars or Saturn was just rising or was at a position directly overhead. There was no explanation, and so a second sampling of the birth times and locations of 508 prominent French medical doctors was gathered. The second sample showed the same statistical correlations with Mars and Saturn.

Gauquelin then made a large survey of professional men in Italy, Germany, Belgium, and Holland, recording 25,000 birth times and locations. The results for physicians were still the same, but the statistics indicated that athletes and military leaders, in addition, all tended to be born under the

Mars or Saturn influence. The figures showed that artists, painters, and musicians were seldom born with the Mars or Saturn positions. Actors or politicians tended to be born when Jupiter was just rising or directly overhead. Gauquelin has published his figures hoping that others will check the correlations in even larger samples.

Since the genes inherited from parents determine many factors in a child's physical makeup, the feeling always has been that heredity helps influence the professions that people choose. Accordingly, Gauquelin decided to see if there was any correlation between heredity and the special planetary relationships. He began by checking the birth times and locations of the parents of those he had surveyed first. There was indeed a relationship. More parents than chance would predict had the same birth patterns as their children, with the same planets in the same locations. The correlation held for either the mother or the father. Furthermore, Gauquelin found that if *both* parents were born when the same planet was rising or overhead, the child was even more likely to be born under the same planetary configuration.

Gauquelin thought that heredity was still very important, but he felt that somehow heredity created an affinity for particular planetary patterns for each individual. The planets, he suggested, simply acted as triggers for the precise hour of birth. The statistics did not fit cases in which the birth timing was changed by artificial means; natural births alone tended to follow the pattern.

Gauquelin found that only the moon, Venus, Mars, Jupiter, and Saturn seemed to have an effect in triggering birth timing. These planetary bodies are the ones that are either closest to the earth or largest in mass, lending support to the idea that some sort of actual gravitational or magnetic field is involved.

New Directions in Astrology

Most of the scientists exploring the effects of sun, moon, and planets on earth life have worked apart from each other at different times and in different places. They are mathematicians, astronomers, physicians, biologists, historians, engineers, and meteorologists. Gauquelin, Piccardi, Jonas, Nelson, and others have found that their special areas of study could be understood fully only by looking beyond the earth to the relationships among the heavenly bodies.

Although these pioneers have been interested in astrology, most of them do not call their science by this name. Instead they use new words like *cosmograms, environmental biology, astrometeorology,* and *gravitational vectoring.* It is true that some of their findings contradict the older ideas of astrology. Some of them, however, show that behind the ancient myths and superstitions about the heavenly bodies have been theories that were sensible and phenomena that can be measured even if not yet well understood.

At the same time that traditional astrology is becoming popular again, a somewhat different scientific "astrology" is developing, in combination with other disciplines, to add to our ever-widening knowledge of our environment.

Index

indicates illustration